OIL RIGS

THE ESSENTIAL GUIDE

BY

COLIN G. HORNBY

OIL RIGS
The Essential Guide

By Colin G. Hornby

© 1997 Colin G. Hornby

First paperback edition 1997

First published in Great Britain in 1997 by
    Books Today
    8 Clegg Avenue
    Thornton Cleveleys
    Lancashire
    FY5 1BJ

The moral right of the author has been asserted

A catalogue record for this book is available from
the British Library

ISBN 1 901667 00 6

Designed by Toni Rose and Richard Farrell, Thornton Cleveleys
Edited by Hedra Hornby
Printed and Bound in Great Britain by
NemcO Press Limited, Preston, Lancs

Acknowledgements

With special thanks to my wife Hedra for her patient efforts in untangling my syntax and grammar! I would like to thank Toni Rose for her invaluable help and advice on putting this project together and I want to thank all my colleagues offshore on the Dunlin Alpha for their interest and help over the last eighteen months.

I am very grateful to my son Geoff for his enthusiastic help and support.

For Hedra, Geoff and Matthew

TABLE OF CONTENTS

INTRODUCTION

Welcome to the first edition of *'OIL RIGS'*. All the information contained in this book has come from people who are involved in the production of oil and gas in the British oilfields.

For many reasons, people seeking work in this industry have found it almost impossible to obtain the correct information. I hope that this book will help you to overcome this problem.

There are many factors at work at the present time that are having an influence on the oil industry in the North Sea, for example: an ageing workforce, which will have to be replaced in the near future. The exploration of marginal oilfields with the latest technology has served to increase the life expectancy of the oilfields well into the next century.

Experience gained in the North Sea can lead to very profitable work overseas as the world demand for oil and gas increases. The industry is in a constant state of evolution and improvement as it tries to meet the demand for these products; it is with this in mind that you should approach the expectation of working offshore.

This book aims to give advice to anyone who is willing to take the step into a well-paid career that involves the individual working for six months of the year (two weeks on, two weeks off). To achieve what may be a complete change of life for oneself, a sense of determination and self-discipline is essential.

This book gives details of the skills involved and the expertise required to bring the oil and gas to the surface.

The intention of this book is to give the reader the advantage of having information on the skills used within the industry. This information will give the future oilfield worker an edge on the competition. The objective is to pick up the information and use it to your advantage. There is no quick fix; however jobs can be acquired by the most determined and disciplined applicants.

It would seem at first sight that there is no place for the unskilled worker. This is not the case as there are certain jobs for people with no skills whatsoever, who can be trained to reach the highest levels of management. This is possibly the only industry in the UK where this can happen. There are people currently running major projects who began their careers by cleaning and sweeping the decks of an offshore drilling rig. This kind of career path is still open to all who by their own efforts can climb the ladder to success.

The industry thrives on individualism, yet it needs people who can work as members of a team because it is only through teamwork that the industry can produce the results demanded by the investment of millions of pounds.

For many centuries, the fishermen had the North Sea to themselves, but by the mid 1970s a new breed of seafarer had taken over; however, they were not looking for fish!

They were after the oil that lay beneath the bed of the North Sea. The rigs appeared individually at first and then in such profusion that they seemed to crowd out all the small fishing boats.

Since 1920 there have been thousands of onshore wells drilled in Europe, the results of which have been disappointing. The Suez crisis in 1956 gave a new boost to secure independent supply in Europe. Natural Gas deposits were found in great profusion in Holland and in realising that the North Sea was geologically the same, exploration started there as well, with good results as far as Natural Gas was concerned.

Some companies continued to explore for oil, though without much enthusiasm. Phillips Petroleum from Bartlesville, Oklahoma was involved in the search, but found nothing. The decision had been made to pull out and cut their losses, however, as they had already paid for the use of the drilling rig (the Ocean Viking) for one more well, they decided to continue because they could not find anyone to hire the rig. The weather was particularly bad that season. The rig lost an anchor and began to drift away from the borehole. The weather was so bad that they were getting ready to evacuate, nevertheless, these problems were overcome and eventually, the Ocean Viking was successful: a well was brought in during November 1969 in to Ekofisk Field. It was a major find. It was what the oil companies were seeking. The race was on for drilling rights!

By the end of 1970, British Petroleum announced the discovery of oil in the Forties Field, 100 miles east of the Ekofisk Field. A series of major strikes followed, including Shell Expro's huge Brent field.

The oil crisis of 1973 turned the exploration in the North Sea into a race. Nothing like this had ever been attempted before by the oil companies and the investment was massive by any standards. The technology was on the leading edge, and the environment was considered to be the worst in the world. The development of the North Sea was one of the greatest investment projects in the world. It was also a technological wonder of the first order, as the platforms had to be built to withstand waves that could reach 100 feet, with wind speeds up to and around 130 miles an hour. It is with this background knowledge that we can view the mature oilfields as they move into the next technological challenge presented by the deeper waters to the west of the Shetlands. The drilling of the deeper wells from the established platforms is a similar challenge.

THE TRADES AND PROFESSIONS INVOLVED IN THE OFFSHORE OILFIELDS

The trades are as one would expect, very similar to the trades carried out in what used to be Britain's heavy plant and machinery manufacturing base: mechanical, electrical and instrumentation, together with engineers in the same disciplines and also welders, riggers and scaffolders. These basic trades are then divided into maintenance, engineering and installation, and then further subdivided into platform, drilling rig, marine and platform personnel.

Platform personnel are usually, but not always, involved with the production of oil and gas. Their work revolves around maintaining production. The person who runs the platform is the offshore installation manager, known by the acronym OIM, whose power is unlimited; therefore it is sound advice to do as they wish. One of the main concerns of the OIM is one of production, allied to safety and another is the management of the platform. The career path for this position starts with a good engineering degree and then training with either production or drilling.

Under the OIM are the safety officers who report directly to the OIM's office. Safety officers can come from any of the disciplines; electrical, mechanical or instrumentation. Their power is considerable and they police the platform with regard to safe working practices. This position would require a good trade qualification and the necessary qualifications in safety management.

The people who run the engineering and production side of the operation would have a degree in their speciality, be it in electrical, mechanical, instrumentation or production engineering. It is not always the case that a degree is required, as we shall see, but major oil companies would seem to demand this level of expertise on their larger platforms, although, there is nothing to stop a person working their way up through further education. In fact, this approach would be positively encouraged. Under these people is a level of supervisors, who would have been promoted from the various trades on the platforms. Everyone works within this type of structure regardless of which department they are working in, be they mechanics, electricians or instrument technicians. The list is quite long, but generally, all the people that would be necessary to run a small town are needed to run an offshore platform or rig. The butcher and baker also have their place on these offshore islands.

There is an entry level at which people without any of the skills or qualifications mentioned above can be employed in the industry and this is:

A Roustabout - Would be working with drilling and this job would be cleaning, assisting on the rig floor, working with the welder as a firewatcher and unloading boats, also all the general jobs required by his foreman. This position requires good eyesight and the ability to understand verbal instructions over the radio and also to be able to understand simple instructions. The roustabout position is the first rung of the ladder up the drilling chain of command.

There is another entry level, for people without vocational or academic qualifications, which is:

Steward: This is on the catering side and is a job requiring various skills and also much energy because it entails a lot of hard work. One of those skills is the ability to run a laundry without losing anyone's clothes! There are several areas on rigs where cups of coffee and tea are dispensed and it is the steward's job to see that they are always kept clean and always have sufficient coffee and tea available. Making the beds, cleaning the showers and rooms, washing up and keeping the galley clean are some of the main jobs. The stewards have an important role in the life of the platform.

PLATFORMS (Fig No. 1)

Platforms are man-made islands which stand on the sea bed. There are many different types, some have three legs and are made of concrete, others are made of steel and have between 6-8 legs. All these structures function in the same manner no matter how many legs they have. Some store oil in the base, others produce to tankers through a system of mooring buoys and some are simply used as pumping stations.

All have one thing in common and that is they are all extremely robust, to enable them to stand up to weather which can sometimes be quite horrendous.

The oil and gas runs up through the structures in the large diameter pipes which come up from the sea bed.

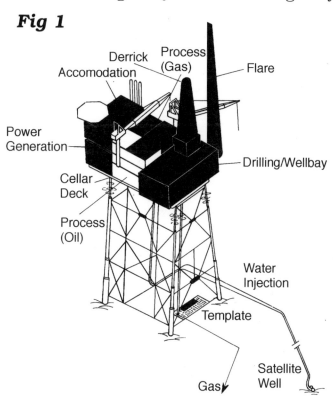

Fig 1

These pipes are called risers and are supported by the main structure until they reach the main production area. It is not uncommon for some of these wells to reach out over 24,000 feet, a distance of 5 miles away from the platform. It is this technology that is still making the North Sea one of the major oilfields in the world. Some of the first generation platforms have a new lease of life with this technology extending their lives for another 10 years or more.

SEMI-SUBMERSIBLES (fig No. 2)

The semi-submersible drilling rig is the workhorse of the North Sea. Its work rate is second to none, no matter what the weather is like. The semi floats, as its name implies, partially submerged, very much like a submarine. It is this ability that gives it the capability to handle the worst the North Sea has to offer. The structure is supported on two pontoons which can be filled or emptied of water; thus raising or lowering the drilling deck to suit the prevailing weather conditions. This process is called ballasting. The reason these rigs handle the weather so well, is due to their low profile to the prevailing wind and sea, because of the supporting pontoons below the water, which make them less susceptible to the large waves than a conventional ship would be.

The rig is kept in position by a system of anchors, usually eight in number, which are laid out by an anchor-handling ship when the rig is moved into its location. To assist in this manoeuvre, the rig has thrusters (propellers) mounted on pontoons which allow the rig crew to have some input into this operation. Some of the more modern units have the ability to move at considerable speed using their own power and so reduce the time it takes to move from location to location; a very important feature, as the rig is usually off the payroll during this time.

The crew of a semi-sub is a small close-knit unit. They work together in extremely difficult conditions to drill wells for the major or minor oil company to which they are contracted. At any one time there will be eighty men on board, working 12 hour shifts. Each shift, generally speaking, being noon until midnight, and midnight until noon. During this 12 hour shift it is not unusual to have only a single 30 minute meal break and two tea or coffee breaks of 15 minutes each—— a very long, hard day!

Semi-subs: operate independently. Should the need arise to abandon the rig, or to pick someone up from the water, support is provided by a small standby vessel. Once a week there will be a supply- boat to bring in supplies of food and water, drilling

Fig 2

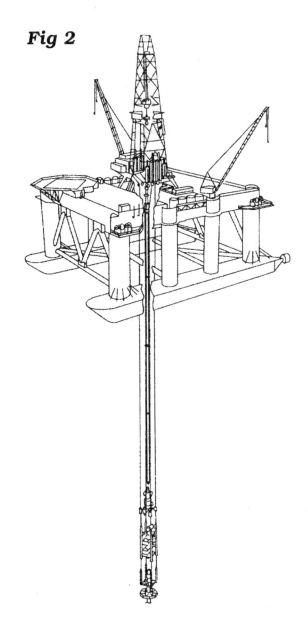

supplies, such as drilling mud, drill pipe or casing.

Semi-subs: tend to move around a lot depending on the wind and sea, but they never get too uncomfortable. There is plenty of room inside the accommodation for recreation space; quiet rooms, gym, sauna and the most popular entertainment − − satellite TV. Videos are also running for 24 hours a day. The difference between the US and European built rigs, is that the European rigs have a little more built-in comfort. Mechanics and electricians generally share accommodation.

Roustabouts and roughnecks also share accommodation in twin cabins. Senior staff, such as; tool pushers and company men (representatives of the company for which the rig is drilling) have a room to themselves.

JACK UP RIGS (Fig No. 3)

The first offshore mobile structure used for exploration in deep water was the jack up rig. One of the first built in Europe was an eight leg unit named the Seashell. The Seashell was built in Holland in 1957, subsequently she spent most of her life as an exploration and workover rig in the Persian Gulf and Arabian Sea.

Jack ups are currently built with three legs and can work in water up to five hundred feet deep.

Fig 3

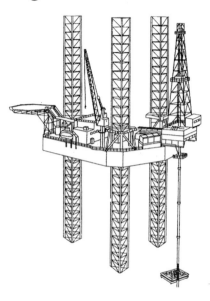

24 motors on each leg operate the jacking system. Each motor operates a gear system that drives a gearwheel, which engages into slots on the leg. Each motor is stopped and started from a central jack-house, where the load on the legs is monitored; each leg being driven independently. The legs are jacked down until they reach the sea bed and it is there, that the base plates penetrate the sea bed. As one leg may penetrate the sea bed more than the others during the operation, the operator will drive each individual leg until the load balances. The rig is then loaded with sea water into ballast tanks and the legs put under tension for 24 hours so that they will settle into the sea bed.

It is at this point that the decision is made to raise the rig to its working position. This point is a critical one. If the decision is made to raise the rig, the operator engages the jacking motors which drive the rig up to a point where there is an air gap of 100 feet between the bottom of the hull and the surface of the sea. The drilling derrick is then moved out on a cantilever mechanism into the drilling position over the sea.

On certain types of jack up the accommodation can be quite cramped. There is a lack of communication to shore as there are not any telephones, so a system of VHF to shore bases is used. Work is hard for the people who work on jack ups, especially for the mechanic and the electrician, because of the amount of equipment involved.

FLOATING PRODUCTION UNITS

Floating production units can either be semi-subs or converted tankers. They are connected to remote wells on the sea bed by an umbilical, heavily armoured, flexible pipe. These floating production units are used in small oilfields where a fixed platform would be far too expensive. They are usually quite comfortable to live on. Obviously the converted tankers have excellent accommodation. Semi-subs are equally as comfortable, in that they do not require a large number of people on board to operate them.

DRILLSHIPS (Fig No. 4)

The drillship is as its name implies, a ship with a drilling derrick in the centre. This type of unit is on the léading edge of technology. They are designed to drill in water depths to a maximum of 5,000 feet. In these depths the ship cannot anchor as the semi-submersible does, it relies on a system of thrusters to maintain its position over the location of the well. The thrusters are run by computers which collate information, such as wind speed and direction. The major mechanism that controls the station keeping is called a 'taut wire device'. It is a heavy weight that sits on the sea bed and is connected to the ship by a wire. The computer then measures the angle of this wire at the ship's side, as

Fig 4

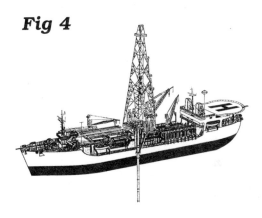

it alters right, left, fore, aft. The corresponding signals are fed to the computer, which tells the thrusters in which way to move the ship to maintain its position. These ships carry a full marine crew and drilling crew. They work together as a team, which is just as well, because this type of work, when it goes wrong, does so very quickly with some amazing results.

Nevertheless, these ships are used internationally, from Brazil to Indo China. These are the rigs to seek work on if you want to travel, because their mobility enables them to sail quickly around the world from job to job. Although these rigs are very expensive to run, they are the only method of drilling in water depths beyond the capabilities of jackups and semi-submersibles at present.

Drill ship crews tend to be a very close-knit team, very professional in outlook and to be found working in some of the more remote parts of the world. One of the main pre-requisites of the crew must be their adaptability to the unpredictability of the wind and sea around them. If you can imagine a ship connected to a sea bed 5,000 feet below them and drilling with this conductor a further 10,000 feet into the sea bed, you can envisage the problems that may arise from mistakes.

Fig 5

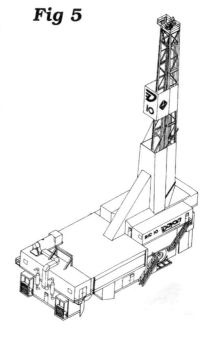

The latest drill ship being built at the moment will have the capability to drill in 11,000 feet of water - a major advancement on the current technology.

LAND RIGS (Fig No. 5)

Land rigs must predominate in any discussion of drilling rigs. They are used all over the world, in all kinds of terrain and weather. Land rigs have existed for 100 years and now they are used widely in the UK and internationally. One of the oilfields in the UK using land rigs is in Dorset, a major project which has been developed continuously for the last 10 - 15 years.

The people who work land rigs in the UK usually stay in hotels, off shift. They still work 12 hour days, working two weeks on, two weeks off, or two weeks on, one week off.

The only people who actually remain on the rig all the time are: the tool pusher, the electrician and the mechanic.

FLOTELS

Flotels, as their names implies, are floating hotels. They are usually converted semi-submersibles, but there are also converted jack ups which are used for accommodation in the southern sector of the North Sea and Morecambe Bay.

Flotels usually accommodate five hundred to eight hundred people and they are anchored alongside the main platform during major projects. Flotels require marine crew to operate them and they also need: engineering, maintenance, electrical, catering systems and radio operators. Flotels are used as accommodation for the contract crews during the refurbishment of old platforms. They are quite comfortable and they have saunas, gymnasiums, quiet rooms, a laundry and a full-sized cinema.

All the personnel who work offshore require statutory basic skills in survival and fire fighting. These are obtained from various institutions around the UK. They tend to be expensive, although one month's pay will more than cover this initial outlay.

You may be thinking at this point, that it appears to be difficult to obtain work within the offshore industry, however, you really will find it easier if you adopt a positive approach. Many offshore personnel have been in the business for 20-25 years and consequently, those members of the work force are nearing retirement and the employment agencies are continually searching for younger staff to fill these openings. The addresses of these agencies are at the end of this book.

THE PEOPLE AND THEIR SKILLS

MECHANICS

Mechanics require a large number of skills. Their most important duties are maintaining the drilling equipment, ordering and looking after spares and new equipment. The equipment that is looked after is generally an up-rated version of that used within mainland British industry; most of the equipment is often of American origin.

One of the primary engines used offshore is the D399 Caterpillar V16, an engine that has been on the market for a long time, but one which is still a very efficient unit. Its output is around 930KW and it is used extensively offshore, not only in the North Sea, but also world-wide. These engines are used to drive the generators that power the drilling unit and as can be imagined, they are extremely robust and reliable. There are usually four to a rig. The cooling system is fresh water, circulating through sea water (the sea water heat exchanger). They are all independent of each other in this respect. Each is controlled by an electrical governor running in the main switch room, where the load on the engines is balanced and the revolutions controlled, at around 1200 rpm. The rig mechanic's work involves the maintenance and repair of hydraulic control systems and also 1600 horse power mud pumps. These are the units that pump the drilling fluid down the drillpipe at a pressure up to 5000 psi. These pumps are driven by two 800 horse power electric motors which have the capability to have their speed and output controlled over a wide range. Hydraulic pumps are used for operating drilling equipment, e.g. lifting, holding, screwing large diameter pipes together.

The use of hydraulic power is increasing within the industry, because it is safe when used in hazardous areas.

Detroit Diesels, manufactured by ALLISON, a division of General

Motors in the United States, are medium-sized engines which are used for pumping cement slurry down the well, to hold the various pipes in place and to pressure test the rigs' drilling systems. They are the standard engine for the drilling industry and are used internationally.

The only other type of drive the mechanic would encounter is an electrical one. Electrically driven screw compressors are the industry standard. The increasing use of computer driven maintenance routines have, in the last few years, become the norm as each rig or platform has to conform to a safety case to satisfy the Health & Safety Executive in that all offshore equipment meets their standards with regard to its operation and maintenance. This has had the effect of increasing the administration workload for the single mechanic running a twelve hour shift.

Rig Mechanics are separate from the main maintenance routine of the platform. They operate in a small unit within the main structure of the platform; in effect a stand-alone unit. They run their own routines, their own administration and have no mechanical supervisor as such. They are responsible for their unit and how it operates. A rig mechanic can at times, experience extreme pressure when things break down. He needs to keep a cool and level head and to make the correct decision at the right time.

Platform Mechanics or 'Clankies' as they are known, are usually employed by a contractor or agency and are sub-contracted to the major oil company. The work is set out by the major oil company and usually involves high speed diesel engines, which are fire pumps, various hydraulic systems, gas turbines for power generation and large export oil pumps of two to three thousand horse power. There are large motor driven valves involved within this production area. Platform mechanics usually work in pairs, as single persons would be unable to raise the alarm if they were injured in a remote location. Platform mechanics operate under a mechanical supervisor and sometimes work possibly two hours overtime a day. They will also be involved with the maintenance of the accommodation:

piping, plumbing, air-conditioning systems and all the general maintenance of the platform that comes under the platform mechanical supervisor. A lot of skill is involved.

Another mechanical skill that is required quite extensively and on every platform, is a Crane Mechanic. Some platforms have five or six cranes. The maintenance of all these systems is the responsibility of the crane mechanic and increasingly, the crane mechanic also has to learn to drive a crane. The industry is rapidly moving into a multi-skilling phase, whereby people need more than one skill.

ELECTRICIANS

Electricians are employed throughout the oil industry on all platforms or offshore units. On the drilling side there is usually one electrician on shift, who works together with a mechanic, to run the power and mechanical systems.

The electrician's responsibilities include the power generation and an SCR system (a Silicon Controlled Rectifier system is a method of converting AC power to a controllable DC voltage). These SCRs drive eight hundred horse power DC drilling motors.

Interfaced with this system would be either a contactor logic or a plc control, (programmable logic controller). The rig electrician's job is not only concerned with power generation and the control of these large DC drives, it also encompasses an instrumentation system which monitors the movement of fluids, temperatures and rate of penetration of drill pipe. On a semi submersible or a jack up the rig electrician is also responsible for all the life support systems, eg air conditioning, the accommodation and galley.

On a platform it is slightly different. Some platforms are supplied by the platform power. A 6kv or an 11kv feeder to transformers, but alternatively, the electricians may have their own power generation as a stand alone unit within the platform.

One of the most important areas that offshore electricians have to operate in, is the electrical hazardous area. The correct installation and maintenance of electrical equipment in hazardous areas is an essential feature of safety.

In order to achieve the desired levels of safety the chain starts with the manufacturer of the electrical apparatus, who has to carry out the necessary and appropriate tests to quality assurance procedures.

The design engineer also has an important role in the correct selection of the electrical apparatus, paying particular attention to the electrical rating, zone classification and prevailing environmental conditions where the apparatus will be installed. Next, the installer must be in possession of all the appropriate documentation, be familiar with the EX-protection concepts and understand the installation codes of practice and wiring regulations.

Whatever National Statutory Safety regulations are in force for a particular type of hazardous area installation, they must be understood and implemented. However, there is a danger of blindly following the regulations without giving some thought to good electrical engineering practice, because regulations can be misinterpreted by individuals. Experience in the UK, following the Piper Alpha disaster, has resulted in engineers seeking certification, or letters from manufacturers confirming that every installation method is covered in writing by a third party and thus relieving them from direct responsibility. This is obviously an impossible situation and engineers must be skilled enough to know that an electrical installation in a hazardous area is safe as far as is reasonably practical.

TRAINING

The following personnel have a particular role to play in accident prevention - managers, foremen, supervisors - they must equally fulfil their duties to provide not only, information and instruction, but also, the necessary training to ensure safety.

The vital role of training and achieving a safe and healthy working environment was recently reviewed by the UK Health & Safety Commission, who, on considering the report on the current and proposed action in the field of health and safety in training, emphasised that, 'workers need to know how to perform their job in a safe way, managers need to have a sound appreciation of the principals of health and safety and its management control. Health and safety professionals are needed to provide specialist advice and support. Due to the fact that information needs to be passed on to employees about hazards and protective measures, and because employees also have duties imposed upon them, many new statutes impose an absolute and legally binding requirement on employers to provide the necessary training.

Absolute or otherwise, the fundamental nature of training and adequate supervision, cannot be over emphasised.

Electrical equipment is therefore, then divided up into different zones, which are:

Zone 0 - An area in which an explosive gas/air mixture is continuously present for long periods.

Zone 1 - An area in which an explosive gas/air mixture is likely to occur in normal operation.

Zone 2 - An area in which an explosive gas/air mixture is not likely to occur in normal operation and if it occurs, will exist only for a short time.

It is within these parameters that the electrician will specify the type of equipment he will put into these areas. It is very important that he follows these rules implicitly.

It is this responsibility that the rig electrician takes on board when he takes the job. There is training available which is quite expensive: however, it would be sponsored by his employer. There at present a course run by Scotia in Aberdeen on electrical equipment in hazardous areas that is essential for all electricians working offshore. There is also, at present, an examination being prepared by Aberdeen University on the installation and maintenance of electrical equipment in hazardous areas, which in future, will become an industry norm for all electricians with the responsibility for this type of equipment.

Rig electricians operate without supervision. There is a toolpusher in charge, but he is not skilled in the electrical or mechanical field, so there are high levels of responsibility for the rig electrician. It is a difficult job technically and sometimes the electrician is under considerable pressure to perform.

The rig electricians work well within their environment. They are usually enthusiastic individuals, who accept the responsibility of the jackup, semi submersible, or the platform with a good nature.

Platform electricians operate within a very tightly controlled structure. They are divided into sections. There is the power technician who is responsible for the power generation on the platform, whose position is becoming increasingly more responsible, as they are often now the responsible person electrical (RPE) and they have to do not only the power technician's job but also have the RPE's job. This work involves not only the production of power, but also responsibility for all the electrical installations. They have to control the electrical work that is taking place on the platform. They are also responsible for all the services within the accommodation and must have, in this position, a very good knowledge of the plant. The power technician will have come from maintenance or engineering and will probably have an HNC or at least a good City & Guilds. It is becoming, as previously stated, an increasingly responsible job.

MAINTENANCE

The platform maintenance electricians are involved with all the platform electrical equipment, from the galley toaster, to the Main Line 500HP pump. They also have to meet the maintenance requirements of the platform EX Hazardous Area Systems. There is a lot of paperwork involved, because every piece of electrical equipment on the platform, down to junction boxes, must be examined at least once a year, depending upon the environmental conditions that they operate in. The job also involves fault finding on various electrical systems on the platform, assisting the RPE in the maintenance of high voltage equipment, the RPE doing the isolations and the maintenance electrician doing the work.

The maintenance electrician would formerly have been employed in the ship yard, iron, coal or steel industries; industries which are disappearing rapidly. The oil industry has used these skills from the British manufacturing base for many years, to augment its own workforce, but unfortunately, since the demise of heavy industrial manufacturing in the UK it is now becoming increasingly difficult to find skilled personnel.

INSTALLATION ELECTRICIANS

Major installations of electrical equipment are carried out by specialist companies, who employ their own electricians for installation and commissioning. They tend to move from job to job, without staying for any considerable time on the platform.

As most new platforms are now built in the construction yards, they are more or less complete when they are shipped offshore. The hook-up is quite straight forward, and requires less staff. In the past, the complete installation was assembled offshore, however, this is no longer done as it is much too expensive.

Installation electricians can earn a good salary on platforms. There are different levels of electrician within the installation framework. Initially, the electrician would be in a cable pulling gang and then would move on to trade work and various other functions of the electrician's trade. The qualification required is a completed apprenticeship and it is at this level that the electrician without any experience in hazardous area equipment can start working in the offshore world. It is a very good learning process in how to work with hazardous area equipment. It is from here that you can move into maintenance engineering or working on drilling rigs. The field is quite open. If you wish to advance yourself by becoming qualified and attending the courses, the salary can be very rewarding.

There is a list of definitions concerning hazardous areas at the back of the book.

INSTRUMENT TECHNICIANS

The instrument technicians are involved in the maintenance of the fire and gas systems, these are both infra-red and smoke. Instrument systems also monitor the process of the production of oil and gas into the export lines. They often monitor environmental conditions. All their equipment operates on a low voltage intrinsically safe system. There has been a move away from the old style pneumatics, although they can still be found on the older platforms.

Closed circuit cameras and monitors also form part of the work of the instrument technicians. The instrument technicians work under the platform management system with the supervisor and the leading technician. To become an offshore instrument technician you require a good City & Guilds or an ONC. There is scope for advancement within this area.

WELDERS

The construction welder deals with all the needs of a construction crew, making major modifications to the plant during shut downs.

The platform welder performs a multi-skilled role; at times a welder, at others a heli-deck assistant, or as part of the deck crew.

The rig welder, on the other hand, continues to fulfil a traditional role as a fabrication welder producing various articles, as and when required.

RIGGERS

Riggers are moving away from their traditional role of lifting and slinging, to a more hi-tech job. This involves being able to use standard climbing equipment, as used in mountaineering, during maintenance and repair work on parts of the platform that would otherwise require very expensive scaffolding. This approach to platform maintenance is widespread and due to cost, is preferred. It is a demanding job that pays well and is open to all those who enjoy climbing and have a skill to sell.

Mechanics and electricians have also been affected by this particular trend of using mountaineering equipment.

SCAFFOLDERS

As the name implies, scaffolders serve the same function offshore as they do onshore. They work in small groups under the supervision of a foreman. When access is required to inaccessible equipment, scaffolders will provide a safe platform to work from. This is a demanding job, which is performed in all weathers.

Scaffolders must work in exposed and dangerous situations. However, this work has to be done and there is a continual demand for this skill.

PRODUCTION TECHNICIANS

Production technicians, as their name implies, control and monitor the production of oil and gas. Their primary function is to fine tune oil wells to maximise production. They do this by monitoring the instrumentation, watching temperatures and pressures, operating first line maintenance: in effect, repairing gauges, belts, compressors and generally keeping things operating efficiently for the maximum oil production. These people are skilled tradesmen who operate to tight production schedules. It is an extremely responsible position with a clearly defined career path.

CONTROL ROOM OPERATORS

All rigs and platforms require control room operators with the ability to read and interpret information from various visual displays and communication devices. The operator usually works alone and not only observes production, but also, oversees the safety panel which monitors the fire and gas sensors placed around the rig. The people who work within this environment are usually skilled tradespeople in their own right. This career is rewarding and can lead to the position of production engineer, which would require some studying for the necessary qualifications in production technology.

DRILLING RIG SUB CONTRACTOR CREWS

A casing crew comes out to the rig when the well that has been drilled needs to be lined with steel pipe. They separate into two crews to work 24 hours a day and stay on the rig until the job is completed. The well is completely lined from top to bottom with steel casing.

Wire line crews are on the rig permanently, specifically on platforms. They operate and run the equipment that affects production of the wells: running tools into the well, on the end of a very fine piece of wire, which open and close downhole valves. Wire line crews also maintain the well heads and 'Christmas trees' (the generic term for the series of valves that control the oil well). The work is very labour intensive and a new employee may work on a variety of platforms or drilling rigs performing various functions concerning oil wells. If your background is electrical then you could find yourself overhauling electrical equipment that is used in the process of oil production, such as: computers, analogue to digital interfaces and also logging information for the drilling engineers to act on. If your background is mechanical then you could find yourself working with the diesel engines and the transmission gear that control the wireline unit.

Wire line crews operate as a team of two or three people; their job is not gender driven. Teamwork is of the essence and there is a very definite career path open to all who can stand the pace.

Logging crews run equipment down into the well to obtain information from the production area; this gives the petroleum and well engineers the data they require to maximise production. It is a very skilled job, the team leader having a degree or similar qualification. Leading a crew of possibly four or five, they run many logs into the well, each one giving the petroleum and well engineers the information that they need.

PLANNERS *(Maintenance and Engineering Inspection)*

Maintenance inspectors and planners have taken on the role of checking and overseeing the work that is done on both disciplines (maintenance and engineering) following the closer involvement of the HSE (Health and Safety Executive) in the running of offshore platforms and rigs. These engineers have a good background in engineering with a sound knowledge of the plant and systems used in the oil industry.

DRILLING RIG CREWS

On nearly all platforms you will find some type of drill crew, it may be a small crew on a care and maintenance basis, or a full crew for drilling oil and gas wells. Crews are comprised of the following people:

TOOLPUSHERS

Toolpushers are in overall charge of the day to day running of the drilling rig. They are also responsible for the health and safety of all the crew members, and are involved in liaising with the company which contracted the crew.

DRILLERS

Drillers run the drill floor, carrying out the instructions they receive from the various specialists involved in the drilling of the well and they are responsible for the safety of the crew on the drill floor. The driller monitors the well for any signs of activity that would suggest a blow out. If this should occur the driller has to activate the safety system to ensure the safety of the rig and personnel involved.

ASSISTANT DRILLERS

Assistant drillers are involved with organising the drilling equipment that comes up to the rig floor and with keeping accurate records of all the drillstring assemblies that are used in the drilling of the well. The assistant driller relieves the driller for meal and coffee breaks.

DERRICKMAN

The derrickman, as the name suggests, looks after the drilling derrick and stows the drillpipe away in the derrick when it is pulled from the well; and also runs the pipe back into the well when required.

The derrickman looks after the mud pumps and the drilling fluids when the rig is drilling, working with the mud engineer in checking and conditioning the drilling mud, so that the drillstring and the wellbore operate at their most efficient level.

ROUGHNECKS

Roughnecks work on the drillfloor, using the various machines to screw the drillpipes and drilling assemblies together. They work in teams of three to four and relieve each other for coffee and meal breaks.

ROUSTABOUTS

Roustabouts work on the pipedeck, organising drillpipe and casing, and all the other various pieces of equipment that are used in the drilling of wells.

Drill crews operate in a linear fashion, each relieving the position on either side of their own position. There is a natural progression of people with the correct aptitude moving through the various positions and gaining in experience as they move up the ladder. These positions are the standard set-up to be found on all drilling rigs, with a few minor variations between platforms and mobile units.

ENGINEERS

The offshore installation manager (OIM) is, in effect, a factory manager who has total control over maintenance and production. It is a graduate entry level that demands an understanding of production and engineering methods as well as good management skills. The ability to handle stress management is vital, as the OIM is responsible for everyone on the platform, and coping with incidents is one of the prime requisites of this position. The OIM of a mobile unit (jack up, semi submersible) does not have the same responsibilities concerning oil and gas production as the OIM of a platform. The main concerns of the OIM are the safety of the rig and good safe working practices amongst the drill crew. The OIM may be an ex-merchant navy captain, chief officer or drilling supervisor.

VARIOUS SPECIALIST CREWS

These jobs are unskilled, and include painting, cleaning and fire watching. There are various companies that specialise in supplying workers for this type of work. It can be dirty and uncomfortable, but working with a good crew can be rewarding. Fire watchers work with the welders and are responsible for looking after the surrounding work place to see that fires do not start, and to prevent any dangerous incidents from intensifying.

MUD ENGINEERS

This job involves monitoring the condition of the drilling fluids. The drilling mud is forced down the well as it is being drilled. This mud must have a hydrostatic head and is kept in the well bore at all times to keep gas or oil at the base of the well. This is to prevent a blow-out.

The mud engineer must have the ability to understand the dynamics of a well during drilling. A degree in chemical engineering and a knowledge of what is happening downhole during drilling are essential. This is an individual who has to work alone and therefore needs to be computer literate, able to write reports and capable of taking important decisions on behalf of the company.

SEAMEN

The oil industry employs a large number of seamen on various types of vessel. There is a standby boat in close vicinity to each platform and rig. It is there as a safety measure, fully crewed at all times and in a constant state of readiness, to assist in any incident, should one occur.

They operate on a 28 days on, 28 days off basis, and the vessel is relieved of its station by another standby boat every month, when it goes for refurbishment. On board the standby boat there are the captain, mate, chief engineer and second engineer, the deck crew who run the safety boat. They are equipped with high speed rescue craft, which are instantly available for rescue or assistance in any weather at any time. Standby boats are usually alongside the platform, within 500 metres. The only time that they leave, is obviously, when they change, or during extremely heavy weather, when they have to dodge the waves downwind of the platform. Most of the people who work on standby boats are ex-trawler men, although there are openings for junior seamen in the use of these high speed rescue craft.

Another type of vessel that is used within the industry is the supply boat. They sail to the platform from the nearest port and they are crewed with a captain, a mate, a chief engineer, a second engineer and a full deck crew. There are opportunities for seamen in the UK who wish to go to sea on standby boats, or supply boats, as an alternative to fishing on trawlers, or to working long voyages in the merchant navy. Marine crews are also required for many different types of sea-going units. These include construction and crane barges, diving support ships and semi submersibles. These vessels operate according to the weather and they are always a good place to start when looking for a job offshore. Dive support ships employ considerable numbers of staff to assist in their operations, as do the construction and pipe lay barges. The work is hard, with a twelve hour shift as the norm and 'sea legs' are required as the sea can get a little rough!

CRANE DRIVERS & MECHANICS

Mechanics are becoming multi-skilled. The lack of training of crane operators in dockyards and heavy steel mills, since the demise of heavy industry within the UK, has brought about a shortage of crane operators. Rig mechanics who used to look after the cranes are now becoming crane operators. It is one of several multi-skilled operations going on throughout the industry.

MEDICS

Medics, obviously, need good nursing qualifications and accident and emergency experience. This job is also becoming increasingly multi -skilled. They must become computer literate, as they now have to run the administration of helicopter movements and they are also involved in the making up of flight lists for crew change; a very important job for all who work in the business.

OFFSHORE EMPLOYMENT

The major oil companies are increasingly moving away from employing their own labour offshore by using contract workers who are employed by various employment agencies, engineering and drilling companies. On any offshore platform there are groups of people with various employers who are all working together on a single project and all moving towards the same goal. Agencies provide the best possible means of finding work when you are seeking a job offshore, but the major oil companies will only employ people for senior positions offshore, a degree being necessary.

LIFE OFFSHORE

Life offshore can be pleasant and quiet, sometimes noisy and frightening. Most offshore platforms have a computer club, fully equipped gym, cinema, very good food - depending on the catering company and also quiz nights. The accommodation is quiet. Due to a no smoking policy on most platforms, smoking is not allowed in the cabins, although there are various areas set aside for smoking. All personnel are issued with personal protective gear - which must be worn, these include: safety spectacles, boots, hard hats and overalls. If prescription spectacles are worn the company will provide these in safety form free of charge. This is the type of equipment that must be worn whenever anybody leaves the accommodation.

There are drills: lifeboat drills, muster drills. Sometimes they are in the morning, sometimes in the evening, sometimes in the middle of the night and it is always advisable when the alarm goes to pick up warm clothing in your room before you go to your muster station. If you do have a safety bag with your survival suit and various other pieces of equipment, take it with you, it is very important - you never know!

Tea points are situated throughout the rigs and at nine o'clock in the morning there may be: sausage rolls, bacon, eggs, depending on what comes out of the galley - in the afternoon it could be cakes! The same happens on nights - at nine o'clock in the evening and three o'clock in the morning.

Most platforms and rigs now have a full satellite TV system installed.

When you come to the end of your trip, there will be a list posted and your flight details noted. You will check in and go through the video brief and safety brief for your helicopter flight.

One very important point that I must stress .... work offshore operates in a very disciplined environment. There are a lot of rules that you must abide by. Breaking these rules, may not only endanger your own life, but can also endanger the life of everyone else.

Work offshore is governed by a permit to work system. This gives the permit controller (PCF), control over all the work that is going on around the platform. Your permit will come from either the control room, or from your supervisor. Each new job has to be submitted 24 hours in advance and will be checked by various responsible people to see if it is in conflict with any other. The permit to work system is an extremely important part of offshore life. A job must be accounted for. These permits must be in position before any job starts and in the event of an incident, they must be able to withstand a critical audit. Companies like Shell send people on a permit user's course for two or three days which gives an overall view of how the permit to work system operates. A permit has to be accepted, signed and signed off when a job is completed. It is not only your own health and safety offshore that is at risk, but also the health and safety of all the other people on the platform.

THE POLICY CONCERNING DRUGS AND ALCOHOL OFFSHORE

All personnel taking up employment in the British oilfields are subject to a full medical examination, including a drugs test, which involves analysis of a urine sample for traces of either hard or soft drugs, e.g. cocaine or cannabis. Any applicant whose test is found positive in respect of banned substances will be informed that their employment is terminated.

Some companies have a random drug testing policy and anyone found positive in this manner would face instant dismissal. Another facet of this policy is implemented during the check in procedure when personnel are going offshore; anyone considered to be under the influence of alcohol or drugs would face their company's disciplinary procedure, which may lead to their dismissal. These policies are rigidly enforced as the safety of everyone is at stake and because the fellow crew members rely on each other to do the right thing at the right time under any circumstances. Many companies have alcohol abuse 'care and support systems' available which can be used by offshore personnel when they are seeking help with this type of problem: this is a completely confidential service.

GRADUATES

There is an increasing demand for graduate engineers, as the major oil companies are opting out of employing them and moving the burden of supplying graduate engineers onto the contracting companies. The contracting companies are being asked to provide an ever increasing number of people with the expertise and knowledge of drilling and production in the oil and gas fields. The contracting companies have responded, together with Aberdeen University, by putting together a new course in drilling engineering technology. Its aim is to offer a graduate an in-depth degree course in the drilling technology that is employed in the oilfield. The course is still in its infancy, but it has been supported by all the leading drilling and service companies.

The successful graduate would gain an MSc in Drilling Engineering, which may lead to a bright career in the drilling and exploration side of the oil business. Commenting in 'The Roustabout' magazine for the oilfield, Dr George Grieg of Aberdeen University said: *'The launch of these new qualifications continue the University's commitment to serving the needs of the oil and gas industry. I am confident that the balanced level of the academic knowledge and industry expertise will ensure the course is a success and more importantly, will help students to develop exciting careers and increased understanding of the industry.'*

GOING OFFSHORE

The check-in time for your helicopter or fixed wing flight is available to you twenty-four hours in advance through your company, it is then your responsibility to arrive at the designated time. Failure to check in at least an hour before departure may mean you miss the flight.

NB: Passengers cannot board the aircraft if they are under the influence of alcohol or drugs.

The three major helicopter companies that operate from Aberdeen are: Bristows, Bond and British International Helicopters. They all operate similar types of aircraft with minor variations, namely: SN 61s, Pumas and Bell 212s. After check-in and before going offshore, all personnel view a video brief of the type, safety systems and procedures of the aircraft in which they will travel. During this check-in procedure some companies may also allocate your offshore room number and bed to you.

Offshore workers wear a survival suit and life-jacket including an inner thermal if flying with Shell (depending on the sea temperature). You should wear shoes over the survival suit. You should keep the survival suit in your cabin during your trip offshore. In the check-in areas of the three companies it is possible to buy newspapers, tea, coffee and snacks. It is the custom for offshore workers to take as many newspapers as possible out to the rigs as there is a shortage of them offshore.

On boarding the helicopter you should check your position in relation to the emergency escapes. You will find after a few flights that you will select instinctively the same seat (the one that you feel most comfortable with) in the aircraft. The majority of people sleep during the flight as conversation is extremely difficult due to noise levels. On some flights there is music over the earphones. It is important to remember that helicopters do not have any toilets on board and a no-smoking policy is in operation on all flights offshore.

The pilot informs the passengers of the flight time to the platform or rig over the intercom and sometimes the aircraft may visit several platforms or rigs en route. It is your responsibility to listen to the instructions given to you by the flight crew as the aircraft approaches your destination.

The helicopter landing crew will unload all the bags and place them in a row on the helideck when you arrive at your destination. The pilot will give the signal to disembark on completion of this operation. The passengers then pick up their bags and follow the instructions of the helideck crew as they clear the helideck.

NB: Do not approach the tail rotors of the helicopter. Do not carry newspapers, books or plastic bags as they can become caught up in the down draught of the rotor blades. Keep away from turning rotors and keep a firm footing as winds across the helideck may be severe.

Remove your lifejacket in the administrative office and pass on to an embarking passenger or helideck crew. Report to the administrative office where the administrator will issue you with a welcome to platform card. This will tell you your cabin number, lifeboat number and Muster Point; and the name of your elected Safety Representative. Keep this card on your person until completion of your offshore shift. Administration will also issue a platform orientation and induction checklist that on completion should be passed through your sponsoring department. Remove your survival suit and store it safely in your cabin for use on your return flight or during shuttling.

Go immediately to your Muster Point and put your identification card on the board. Study the station bill in detail and familiarise yourself with the various station lights and determine from it the actions required by you in the event of an emergency. If you are unsure about anything to do with the station bill you should see your supervisor straight away.

Your supervisor will conduct you on a tour of the important points on the platform, for example; Muster and lifeboat stations and the quickest route between them, the safety office, stores, etc.

If this is your first visit you should attend a platform induction course soon after your arrival. Your supervisor will advise you of the time and show you the place on your conducted tour.

If your doctor has prescribed drugs for you then you should report this to the medic as soon as possible after arriving; and you should inform him if you have any allergies.

You may have a cabin allocated to you on an accommodation vessel either alongside the installation on which you are working or alongside another platform in the field. In either case, you should receive specific instructions on your arrival.

WHAT YOU NEED TO TAKE OFFSHORE

You must have a valid passport and you are also required to have taken a medical examination which passed you fit for at least the duration of your visit offshore.

A certificate of attendance at an RGIT combined survival, firefighting and first aid course, or equivalent is mandatory.

OFFSHORE WORKING EQUIPMENT AND CLOTHING

(1)   Safety helmet with chin strap,

(2)   Flame retardant overalls or coveralls particular to your trade,

(3)   Approved safety footwear,

(4)   Protective goggles-spectacles,

(5)   Ear protection - it is a disciplinary offence to enter a high noise area without using adequate hearing protection,

(6)   The first four items must be worn outside the accommodation areas and must be in good condition. The other items are required according to the type of job or area you work.

You will also need warm clothing in case of cold weather. Remember, two or three layers of thinner clothing provide better warmth than one thicker item.

When travelling to and from the platform you will be provided with a survival suit. Your shoes, which should be loose fitting with non-slip soles, must be worn outside this suit. Footwear for the accommodation area must be clean. The trainer type shoe is recommended.

PERMITTED ITEMS

You are permitted to take the following items but they are only to be used in the accommodation area:

(1)   Electric Shaver - Shaving points are provided in all cabins.

(2)   Calculator

(3)   Camera - Written permission for use must be obtained by the OIM. Use is normally restricted to the accommodation area but special permission may be obtained for work area photography. Strict rules also apply to the use of flashguns on installations.

NOTE: **Radio/cassette music is provided in the cabins.**

PROHIBITED ITEMS

You are **NOT** allowed to take any of the following items to the installation:

(1)   Alcohol,

(2)   Drugs, unless accompanied by written proof from your doctor that they are prescribed for you,

(3)   Weapons of any description,

(4)   Gas cylinders,

(5)   Aerosols,

(6)   Cigarette lighters of any kind and lighter refills,

(7)   Matches,

(8)   Flammable items,

(9)   Toxic/Corrosive/Chemical items (including mercury),

(10) CB radios,

(11) Radioactive substances,

(12) Explosives,

(13) Poisons,

(14) Magnetic materials.

BAGGAGE

You will need a holdall type bag for your personal possessions, suitcases are not advised. Try to keep your luggage to one item.

MONEY

Do not carry a large sum of money offshore. Cheques supported by a bank card, are acceptable for any purchased articles.

PRODUCING A CV

CVs can be used for various purposes.

1. Applying for advertised positions if the employer specifies that the applicants must send in a CV.

2. Applying for possible positions. If there are no current positions, your CV can be a lasting record of your details.

3. By employment agencies, when they are forwarding your name to employers on their books.

4. As an aid in completing application forms.

5. For general purposes when you are self-employed, etc.

6. As a personal introduction to companies or banks when you need to explain your background for some reason. Once you have produced a CV, you will have a big advantage over many other job seekers, in that you are ready to apply for a job when one becomes available. Sometimes there may be some aspects of your career history that you are not content with. Although it would be wrong to lie about your details, there are some ways of accentuating the things that you are proud of.

THE RULES

- **Keep it simple**
- **Make it clear**
- **Keep it short.**

Divide into six different sections:

1. Personal details
2. Education and qualifications
3. Employment
4. Interests and hobbies.
5. Additional information - details of other skills or type of work wanted.
6. References - names and addresses of two people who will give character references for you.

The aims of a CV are to accentuate the good points of your experience and skills and play down any disadvantages in your work history.

CVs should ideally be restricted to two sides of A4.

CONTENT

One way to make sure your CV is noticed by a prospective employer is to make it very obvious if you have done anything unusual. Your CV may be noticed by the employer simply because there is something different about it that makes you stand out from all the others. If you can describe some unusual activity that other people may not have taken part in, you will appear to have had different experience from others and therefore to an employer you may be worth employing.

At this stage let us try and find out what material should be put in a CV.

PERSONAL DETAILS

This section is easy to put together. It is just about the factual details of your life - names, addresses and telephone numbers are placed at the beginning so that your name and means of contacting you cannot be overlooked.

NAMES are written as 'John Smith'.

MIDDLE names are not necessary.

SURNAMES should come at the end.

'J. R. Smith' should be avoided as it will be hard for an employer to remember.

ADDRESS: Always use your postcode and full address.

TELEPHONE: Always remember to include your telephone number. If you are not on the telephone try to find a friend or relative whose number you can use.

(as long as you are sure messages will be taken reliably)

(Put the full STD code and number, eg 01224 121212)

DATE OF BIRTH: 2 March 1967 looks clearer than 02.03.67, or 02/03/67.

Always use your date of birth rather than your age, otherwise it will have to be updated annually.

Always enter your date of birth because an employer will be interested in your age.

NATIONALITY: This aspect of your personal details is very important. If you are from another country it is essential for you to specify that you have a full UK Work Permit.

EDUCATION: This section is for you to outline your educational history, from secondary school onwards.

The information needed first are the dates that you attended your secondary school.

Next the name and location of the school(s) should be included the whole address not being necessary.

The last piece of information is any examinations passed or, if none were taken, the subjects studied. Do not put down failed subjects. If in certain subjects you have obtained distinctions, scholarships or prizes, include this information as it will also set you apart from other candidates. Details about college should be given in the same way, following school details.

EMPLOYMENT: This part encompasses the different jobs you have done. Research all the starting and finishing dates of all the various jobs you have done, including part-time, holiday and voluntary jobs, if you haven't had much employment experience. Include either just the year, or both the month and the year, appropriate to each position. If you have had many jobs, or have gaps between jobs that you would like to 'smooth over', then just the year may be appropriate.

For this part, reverse the order of your employment history. Start with your most recent job and list them all, ending up with your first employment; the reason being, because the job in which you had the most responsibility (normally your last) will come first on the list.

The main difference between this part and the last is that you need to say what the job title was in each case and also to specify the duties of each job.

Try to think of all the things that you did in each job and list them all before you start to write the details. Make sure that you mention at the beginning of your list of duties whether you were in charge of other people. Include any promotions that you achieved.

Do not include details about why you left each job, or what salary you earned in each position.

INTERESTS: Your interests show that you have a well-rounded personality and do not live for work alone. Interests that you have, or have had in the past that are unusual will help you stand out. If you mention some physical activities, as well as some cultural ones, it will show that you are a lively, healthy and active person. Employers often select your hobbies as an easy area of questioning, so try not to let your imagination run away with you- be truthful.

ADDITIONAL INFORMATION: This part can be very important for those with gaps in the other sections of their CV. If you have travelled widely you can write about it here. This is your chance to explain why you are interested in a new type of work, if you are changing career direction.

This is usually written out in full.

If you have particular skills that are relevant, you can include them here, e.g. driving licence, car ownership, first aid, ability on computers, word processing skills, ownership of a computer, etc.

REFERENCES: You should name here two people who can be approached to provide a reference for you. One should be your last employer, or someone from your last school or college and the other should be a friend.

You cannot afford to have an employer contact someone whose name you have given as a reference only to be told that he or she does not want to vouch for you. Character referees should normally have a good job of their own and must not be in your own family. Family doctors or priests can often be approached if they have known you for some time, but you must get their permission first.

Include a telephone number for both referees if possible, although check first that this is acceptable to your referees.

LAYOUT: There are certain features about your CV that will jump out at the reader. The main one is your name. If the employer is sifting through a pile of 20 CVs, you must make sure that your name is easy to spot. If you can use a word processor, put your name in bold. If typed, underline or double type it.

Other details to be emphasised are the level of exams that you have taken and the position of each job that you have held.

Do not emphasise the words curriculum vitae. You also do not need to emphasise the sub-headings of 'Name', 'Address', etc.

DO'S AND DON'TS

DO	keep it simple, avoid long words, etc.
DO	make it clear, easy to understand.
DO	keep it short, two pages maximum if possible.
DO	be positive - accentuate what was achieved in any certain situation.
DO	assume that the reader does not know what you did in your different jobs.
DO	take time to put your CV together.
DO	get to know your CV inside out.
DO	get the finished product word processed, if at all possible.
DO	update your CV whenever you have new experiences, qualifications, etc.
DON'T	use jargon or slang.
DON'T	use pretentious language - write simply and clearly.
DON'T	copy someone else's CV.
DON'T	invent information.
DON'T	lie about yourself.

DON'T   worry about boasting about yourself.

DON'T   send out the original of your CV. It may be difficult to get copies.

DON'T   run out of copies to send out.

AN EXAMPLE OF A CV

Name:

Address:

Telephone Number:

Date of Birth:

Nationality:

Marital Status:

___

EDUCATION

(Subheadings:)

Dates	Name & Locations	Qualifications or Subjects Studied

___

EMPLOYMENT

(Subheadings:)

Dates	Name & Locations	Position Held and Main Duties

___

OTHER SKILLS

___

INTERESTS

___

ADDITIONAL INFORMATION

___

REFERENCES

THE FUTURE FOR THE OFFSHORE INDUSTRY

The future for the UK offshore industry seems bright at the moment with massive investment to the west of the Shetlands, older platforms being refurbished in the East Shetland Basin (and elsewhere) and continuing projects in Morecambe Bay and Liverpool Bay. People with skills are needed for all of these projects, especially within the electrical and electronic fields. A knowledge of electronics is becoming increasingly more useful as the plc (programmable logic controller) and the computer play a more important role in running plant and equipment. Welders and riggers are becoming multi-skilled, because platforms in the future will be working at minimum manning levels. The ability to do more than one job will be a distinct advantage.

There are major oil companies that are moving towards a stand alone policy. This is, in effect, a single self managing unit that runs itself, with the workforce empowered to make changes within its own structure to generate wealth. This could lead to a profit sharing scheme which all the members of the platform team would share.

The future prospects for the employee who seeks further education, particularly in the contract drilling area are very good. There is a realisation, that employees who are well educated can be used as a marketing tool in the search for new contracts by their employers.

It is worth keeping this in mind when you take that job at base level, as the prospects are good for people who are willing to work, not only with their hands, but also with their minds.

CONCLUSION

You may have come to the conclusion after reading this book, that a job in the British oilfields is beyond your reach. Nothing could be further from the truth because with dedication and the will to succeed, the job that you want can be yours.

The oil companies need new people to replace the ageing workforce that is in place at the moment. One point you ought to remember though, is to aim your skills at the correct agencies and companies. The shotgun approach to the business of finding that job may sometimes succeed, but the most effective method is to direct your energies towards the companies that you know will match your skills.

Don't be afraid to speak to these people on the telephone. Make a positive nuisance of yourself! Get your name known. The persistent and assertive approach to finding that job will pay off in the end so if asked, 'do you know or have you worked on this piece of equipment in the past?' Always be positive; and then go and find out the answer. The use of jargon within the industry can be off-putting, but you should not be afraid to ask people what they mean.

In this book I have tried to give the potential offshore worker some guidance into finding a way through the maze of offshore employment, the skills required and a clearer view of what it is like to work offshore.

The ball is now in your court!   I wish you well. Good luck!!

ADDRESSES

DRILLING CONTRACTORS

The drilling contractors below employ all the trades and they are the companies that the person wishing to be a roustabout should apply to.

Notes

Deutag Drilling
Minto Drive
Altens
Aberdeen
Telephone: 01224 295800

Dolphin Drilling Limited
Howmoss Drive
Kirkhill Industrial Estate
Dyce, Aberdeen
Telephone: 01224 411411

ENSCO Offshore UK Limited
Ensco House
Badentoy Avenue
Port Lethen, Aberdeen.
Telephone: 01224 780400

Foramac Drilling Limited
Unit 1, Ticehill Base
Craigshaw Crescent
West Tullis, Aberdeen
Telephone: 01224 899448

Global Marine
Drilling Company
North Norfolk House
Pitmedden Road
Dyce, Aberdeen
Telephone: 01224 246900

KCA Drilling Limited
Minto Drive
Altens
Aberdeen
Telephone: 01224 299600

Maersk Company Limited
Unit 1, Pitmedden
Industrial Estate
Pitmedden Road
Dyce
Aberdeen
Telephone: 01224 771161

Nabors Drilling &
Energy Services
Kirktown Avenue
Pitmedden Road
Industrial Estate
Dyce
Aberdeen
Telephone: 01224 770077

Notes

NEDDRILL UK Limited
Woodbase
Sinclair Road
Aberdeen
Telephone: 01224 898988

Reading - Bates UK Limited
Stoney Wood Business Park
Stoney Wood Road
Dyce
Aberdeen
Telephone: 01224 285600

Rowan Drilling UK Limited
Seaforth Centre
30 Waterloo Quay
Aberdeen
Telephone: 01224 586262

Santa Fe Drilling Company
(North Sea) Limited
Greenbank Crescent
East Tullos
Aberdeen
Telephone: 01224 404200

SEDCO-FOREX
Craigshaw Road
Aberdeen
Telephone: 01224 230500

Notes

Smedvig Limited
HarenessRoad
Altens Industrial Estate
Altens
Aberdeen
Telephone: 01224 246000

SONAT Offshore
(UK) Incorporated
Hareness Circle
Altens
Aberdeen
Telephone: 01224 414700

Stena Drilling Limited
Greenbank Crescent
East Tullos
Aberdeen
Telephone: 01224 401180

Trans Ocean Drilling
Contractors Limited
Denmore Road
Denmore Industrial Estate
Bridge of Don
Aberdeen
Telephone: 01224 704848

Notes

EMPLOYMENT AGENCIES

All trades and professions.   *Notes*

Aker Oil and Gas
Technology UK plc
Aker House
Blackness Road
Altens
Aberdeen
AB1 4LH
Telephone: 01224 890905

Aquatic Engineering
& Construction Ltd
Palmerston Centre
29/31 Palmerston Road
Aberdeen
AB1 2QP
Telephone: 01224 573359

Bryant Engineering Services
Limited
Bryant House
440 Union Street
Aberdeen
AB1 1TR
Telephone: 01224 643736

Data Marine Systems Ltd
Data Marine House
Stoneywood Park
Dyce
Aberdeen
AB2 0DF
Telephone: 01224 725133

East Anglian Electronics Ltd
Unit 3, Wellheads Way
Dyce Industrial Park
Dyce
Aberdeen
AB2 0GD
Telephone: 01224 725552

Fircroft Engineering Services
(Northern) Ltd
480 Union Street
Aberdeen
AB1 1TS
Telephone: 01224 622702

GSR Engineering Limited
3 Rubislaw Terrace
Aberdeen
AB1 1XE
Telephone: 01224 626462

Genesis Personnel
79 Broad Street
Peterhead
Grampian
AB42 6JL
Telephone: 01779 476311

Ken Basey
Engineering Services
97 Hutcheon Low Drive
Persley
Aberdeen
AB2 2WD
Telephone: 01224 692912

Kvaerner Professional
Services Limited
5-9 Hadden Street
Aberdeen
AB1 2NU
Telephone: 01224 575110

L.A. Recruitment &
Management Services Ltd
9 Holburn Street
Aberdeen
AB1 6BS
Telephone: 01224 574215

Lawrence Allison Services Ltd
Trafalgar House
Hareness Road
Altens
Aberdeen
AB9 2PB
Telephone: 01224 400045

McPherson Associates
1/3 Little Belmont Street
Aberdeen
AB1 1JG
Telephone: 01224 646809

Moody International Ltd
Unit 3, Saxbone Centre
Howe Moss Crescent
Kirkhill Industrial Estate
Dyce
Aberdeen
AB2 0GN
Telephone: 01224 771199

Notes

Morgan Moore Eng. Ltd
Altec Centre
Unit 2 & 3, Minto Drive
Altens
Aberdeen, AB1 4LW
Telephone: 01224 248248

Onstream Ltd
Top Floor Suite
461 Union Street
Aberdeen
AB1 2DB
Telephone: 01224 574483

Parc Apollo Technical Services
2A Rose Street
Aberdeen
AB1 1UA
Telephone: Aberdeen 649649

RTD (UK) Ltd
Hareness Circle
Altens Industrial Estate
Aberdeen
AB1 4LY
Telephone: 01224 890010

Rigman Offshore (UK) Ltd
5A Wellheads Crescent
Dyce
Aberdeen, AB2 0GA
Telephone: 01224 725532

Roevin Management
Services Ltd
43 Dee Street
Aberdeen
AB1 2DY
Telephone: 01224 572852

Rotech Fabrication Ltd
Whitemyres Avenue
Mastrick Industrial Estate
Aberdeen
AB2 6HQ
Telephone: 01224 698698

TA Engineering Services Ltd
Badentoy Avenue
Portlethen
Aberdeen
AB1 4YB
Telephone: 01224 780790

John Wood Group PLC
John Wood House
Greenwell Road
Aberdeen
AB1 4AX
Telephone: 01224 851000

CONSTRUCTION COMPANIES

AOC International Ltd
Alba Gate
Stoneywood Park
Dyce
Aberdeen, AB2 0HN
Telephone: 01224 770033

Atlantic Power & Gas Ltd
Salvesen Tower
Blaikies Quay
Aberdeen
AB1 2PW
Telephone: 01224 259500

Brumac Engineering Ltd
Palmerston House
221 Market Street
Aberdeen
AB1 2PT
Telephone: 01224 212345

Deborah Services Ltd
Offshore Division
Hareness Road
Altens Industrial Estate
Aberdeen, AB1 4LE
Telephone: 01224 890790

Dietsmann (UK) Ltd
Thistle Road
Aberdeen Airport
Dyce
Aberdeen, AB2 0NN
Telephone: 01224 770353

GSR Engineering Ltd
3 Rubislaw Terrace
Aberdeen
AB1 1XE
Telephone: 01224 626462

Lawrence Allison Services Ltd
Trafalgar House
Hareness Road
Altens
Aberdeen, AB9 2PB
Telephone: 01224 400045

CATERING

The companies listed below will take people with no offshore experience as long as they hold a current survival certificate.

Notes

Chalk Catering
52 Carden Place
Aberdeen
AB1 1UP
Telephone: 01224 640451

CCG (UK) Ltd
Guild Street
Aberdeen
Telephone: 01224 211051

Kelvin International Services
5 Queens Terrace
Aberdeen
Telephone:
01224 640124/640649

OIL COMPANIES

The oil companies do tend to take on graduates and well qualified engineers.

Notes

Amerada Hess Ltd
Scott House
Hareness Road
Altens
Aberdeen
Telephone: 01224 243000

Amoco (UK) Exploration Co
Greenbank Road
Aberdeen
Telphone: 01224 871041

Hornbeck Offshore Ltd
7-13 South Esplanade West
Aberdeen
AB1 3AA
Telephone: 01224 871777

Lasmo North Sea Plc
Belmont House
1 Berry Street
Aberdeen
Telephone: 01224 842500

Marathon Oil (UK) Ltd
Marathon House
Anderson Drive
Aberdeen
Telephone: 01224 803000

Midland & Scottish
Resources plc
Crawpeel Road
Altens
Aberdeen
Telephone:
01224 878218/876113

Mobil North Sea Ltd
Sage Terminal
St. Fergus
Peterhead
Telephone: 01779 876300

Phillips Petroleum Co. UK Ltd
Regent Centre
Regent Road
Aberdeen
Telephone: 01224 576155

Shell U.K. Exploration
and Production,
1 Altens Farm Road
Nigg
Aberdeen
Telephone: 01224 882000

Sun Oil Britain Ltd
Sun Oil House
25 Union Terrace
Aberdeen
Telephone: 01224 64610

MARINE COMPANIES

Notes

C-MAR SERVICES (UK) Ltd
3rd Floor
Union Buildings
15 Union Street
Aberdeen
AB1 2BU
Telephone: 01224 572832

McDermott Marine
Construction Ltd
Blenheim House
Fountainhall Road
Aberdeen, AB2 4DT
Telephone: 01224 615200

Maersk Supply Service
Unit 1
Pitmedden Road
Dyce
Aberdeen
AB2 0DP
Telephone: 01224 725858

Nomis Shipping Ltd
186 Albert Quay
Aberdeen
AB1 2QA
Telephone: 01224 210383

Star Offshore Services Marine Limited

6 Albyn Terrace

Aberdeen

AB1 1YP

Telephone: 01224 645345

Notes

ESSENTIAL READING

Notes

The Grampian
Business Directory
Distribution Department,
Aberdeen Teleworking
Centre Ltd
105 Victoria Road
Aberdeen
AB1 3LX
Telephone: 01224 875532

Press and Journal
P O Box 43
Lang Stracht
Mastrick
Aberdeen
AB15 6DF
Telephone: 01224 690222

Roustabout Publications Ltd
Suite 5
International Base
Greenwell Road
East Tullos
Aberdeen, AB12 3AX
Telephone: 01224 876582

NB: the Grampian Business Directory is an in-depth look into all the companies operating in the North Sea. It is packed full of information concerning their activities. The Press and Journal is Aberdeen's local evening newspaper and has a large oilfield job section in the Friday edition and finally, the Roustabout magazine is a general overview of the oilfield's techniques and equipment used.

ACRONYMS

During the course of your time offshore you may come across a large number of acronyms and are perhaps unsure what they mean. Below is a selection of relevant ones which may prove useful.

AAT	Area Accountable Technician
AGT	Authorised Gas Tester
ALARP	As Low as Reasonably Practicable
ALQ	Additional Living Quarters
AO	Asset Owner
APS	Authorised Permit Signatory
BCF	Bromochlorodifluoromethane (Halon 1211- hand held appliances)
BGCP	Break-Glass Call Point
CCR	Central Control Room
CDS	Chemical Data Sheet
COSHH	Control of Substances Hazardous to Health
CWP	Cold Work Permit
ERB	Emergency Response Base
ERR	Emergency Response Room
ESD	Emergency Shut Down
ESR	Emergency Safety Representative
F&G	Fire and Gas
GPA	General Platform Alarm
HEL	Higher Explosive Limit
HC	Hydrocarbons
HV	High Voltage
HVAC	Heating, Ventilation and Air Conditioning
HWP	Hot Work Permit
ISO	Installation Safety Officer
IST	Installation Safety Technician
LEL	Lower Explosive Limit

LSA	Low Specific Activity
OIM	Offshore Installation Manager
OIS	Offshore Installation Supervisor
PA	Public Address
PAPA	Prepare to Abandon Platform Alarm
PC	Platform Co-ordinator
PCF	Platform Co-ordination Facility
PCM	Physical Condition Monitoring
PCR	Process Control Room
PFP	Passive Fire Protection
PICWS	Person In Charge of the Worksite
PINS	Permit Information System
PLQ	Personnel Living Quarters
POPM	Platform Operating Procedures Manual
PPE	Personal Protective Equipment
PRC	Preparation and Reinstatement Certificate
PSB	Proactive Safe Behaviour
PSL	Platform Status Lights
PTW	Permit to Work
SMS	Safety Management System
SPS	Surface Process Shutdown
SRB	Sulphate Reducing Bacteria
SS(P)	System Supervisor (Process)
STEL	Short Term Exposure Limit
TBT	Tool Box Talk
TR	Temporary Refuge

HAZARDOUS AREAS - Definitions and Terms

HAZARDOUS AREA:

An area in which explosive gas/air mixtures are likely to be present in such quantities as to require special precautions for the construction and use of electrical apparatus.

IGNITION TEMPERATURE:

The lowest temperature of a flammable gas or vapour at which ignition occurs under test conditions.

INTRINSIC SAFETY:

A protection concept in that no spark or thermal energy is capable of causing the emission of given explosive atmosphere.

LPG - LIQUEFIED PETROLEUM GAS:

A flammable gas is derived from hydrocarbons stored at high pressure that liquefies the gas.

AMBIENT TEMPERATURE:

The temperature of air or other medium where electrical apparatus is to be used.

AREA CLASSIFICATION:

The classification of an area according to the probability of an explosive mixture being present.

ELECTRICAL APPARATUS:

The combination of electrical components that have been tested and certified to form a piece of apparatus suitable for use in hazardous areas.

APPARATUS GROUP:

The Gas Group assigned to the electrical apparatus to indicate its suitability for use in hazardous areas.

BASEEFA (BRITISH APPROVAL SERVICE FOR ELECTRICAL EQUIPMENT FLAMMABLE ATMOSPHERES):

A division of EECS, Electrical Equipment Certification Service.

BONDING CONDUCTOR:

A protective conductor providing equally potential bonding, normally to earth.

CABLE GLAND:

An entry component with electrical enclosures to maintain its specified design and ingress protection, integrity and to provide a means of connecting the cable or screen.

CERTIFICATION:

Verification by a recognised Test Authority that a piece of electrical apparatus has been tested and complies with the appropriate standard.

CREEPAGE DISTANCE:

The shortest distance over the surface of an insulation between the live parts and live parts to earth.

CLEARANCE DISTANCE:

The shortest distance in air between live parts and live parts to earth.

COMPARATIVE TRACKING INDEX - CTI:

A value grading - the resistance to tracking for an insulation material.

COMPONENT SPECIFICATION:

A formal test by a recognised Test Authority that a product complies with an appropriate standard.

EARTH:

The conducting mass earth, that may be soil or similar, where electrical potential is conventionally taken to zero.

ELECTRICAL PROTECTION:

The measures applied to circuits to control the effect over current of an earth fault.

ENCLOSURE:

A part providing an appropriate degree of protection for electrical components against contact with live parts.

EQUAL POTENTIAL BONDING:

Electrical connection to maintain various exposed conductive parts at a substantially equal potential within a safe touch voltage limit.

EXPLOSIVE ATMOSPHERE:

A mixture with air under atmospheric conditions of flammable substances in the form of gas or vapour, in such proportions that it can explode in contact with arcs, sparks or excessive temperature.

EX PROTECTION:

The measures applied to electrical apparatus to prevent ignition of a surrounding explosive mixture.

EXPLOSION LIMITS:

The upper and lower concentrations of gas above and below which an explosion mixture will not be formed. Expressed UEL & LEL.

EXPLOSION PROOF ENCLOSURES:

The North American term for flameproof enclosures, ie an enclosure that is designed to withstand the internal pressures of an explosion without transmission of flames to the external atmosphere.

FLAMMABLE MIST:

A free suspension of droplets of a liquid in which the vapour is flammable.

FLAMMABLE GAS:

Derives from a flammable material, of which boiling point at normal pressure is below ambient temperature.

FLASHPOINT:

The minimum temperature at which a material gives off sufficient vapour to form an explosive atmosphere.

GAS GROUPING:

A method of grouping gasses relative to ignition energy and specific gravity.

HAZARDOUS:

The presence, or the risk of presence, of explosive gas/air mixture.

MARKING:

The labelling of EX Protected Electrical components and apparatus indicating the manufacture, product type, type of EX protection, Test Authority and Certificate number, etc.

MESG - Maximum Experimental Safe Guard:

Is the maximum gap in millimetres for a 25mm flame path of flameproof apparatus, that will not propagate an internal explosion through the flame path.

MIC - Minimum Ignition Current:

Is the minimum in an inductive spark to ignite the most explosive gas/air mixture.

MIE - Minimum Ignition Energy:

Is the minimum energy required from a spark discharge to ignite a specified gas/air mixture expressed in microjoules.

MIT - Minimum Ignition Temperature:

The lowest temperature at which the gas/air mixture will ignite spontaneously.

PRESSURE PILING:

An increase in explosion pressure caused by pre-compression of the gas/air mixture prior to ignition.

PRESSURISATION:

A method of EX protection for electrical apparatus.

EEXP:

Whether either clean air or an inert gas is used to maintain a pressure in an enclosure above atmospheric pressure with a minimum over pressure of 0.05 kilo pascal.

PURGING:

The method of ensuring that a pressurised enclosure is free of any gas prior to energisation of the electrical system.   Purging can be either with clean air or an inert gas. Each system would have a pressure and time cycles specified.

SHUNT & DIODE BARRIERS:

A safety interface device that is designed to divert excess energy from reaching the Hazardous Area.

STORED ENERGY:

The electrical energy stored in an electrical system and by inductance or capacitance that could produce an incentive spark with sufficient energy to ignite the gas/air mixture.

TEMPERATURE CLASSIFICATION:

The maximum surface temperature that certified piece of EX protected electrical apparatus will reach under the most onerous conditions relative to the ambient temperature of 40°C normally.

TEST AUTHORITY:

Recognised Test Houses for certification of EX protected electrical components and apparatus.

TYPES OF EX PROTECTION:

The different explosion protection concepts apply to electrical apparatus, e.g. flameproof - EEXD; increased safety - EEXE; intrinsic safety - EEXI.

UL - Underwriters Laboratories:

They are the American approval bodies.

UFL - Upper Flammable Limit:

A mixture of gas/air where a percentage of gas is too high to be ignited.

ZONE CLASSIFICATION:

A method of classifying Hazardous Areas according to the presence and type of concentration of explosive gas/air mixture.